CASA
MEDITERRANEA

Mediterranean Sea

SEA FORCE ONE

Designed by Luca Dini Design, built by Admiral Mariotti Yachts

Preceding pages:
Page 1 The upholstered chair with a folding eye-shaped back was designed by Captain Magic. *Pages 2–3* In the TV area of the main deck, a mirror set into a slate slab conceals the television. The plexiglas chest is by Paul Smith. The metal sculpture, *The Piratess*, is by Carlo Lombardi and Roberto Vannucci.

Right The main saloon has backlit Barrisol walls. Mai-Thu Perret's work *Big Golden Rock* is in the foreground, and Plessi's video sculpture can be seen behind it.

The large new yacht *Admiral 54 Sea Force One*, whose owner has adopted the identity of the superhero Captain Magic, is a veritable floating home and a Neverland for eternal Peter Pans. At 54 metres (177 feet) long and 10.5 metres (34 feet) wide, with four decks, five passenger cabins and twelve crew members, it is truly a unique and spectacular boat. The innovative materials and the advanced technologies used in its construction, together with the designer objects and works of art on board, make it a perfect link between land and sea – a superbly well-equipped slice of stability on the high seas. In short, it is a perfect starting point for our voyage of discovery through Mediterranean architecture.

Above In the main saloon, a video sculpture by Fabrizio Plessi is reflected on the flat surface of the showcase table, which contains Kiki Smith's artwork *Untitled (Bones)*.

Above The foyer of the main deck. The wall is covered with a mother-of-pearl mosaic from Antolini Luigi. At the bottom of the steel and plexiglas staircase is a bronze sculpture in the shape of a gigantic fish hook.

Left The headboard in the master suite, representing a coral reef, was made by Carlo Lombardi and Roberto Vannucci using plaster and papier mâché. The wardrobe has mirrored doors.

The upper deck saloon has a leather floor and a polycarbonate ceiling. A mobile bar with wide-screen TV can be seen on the left, and a DJ console on the right.

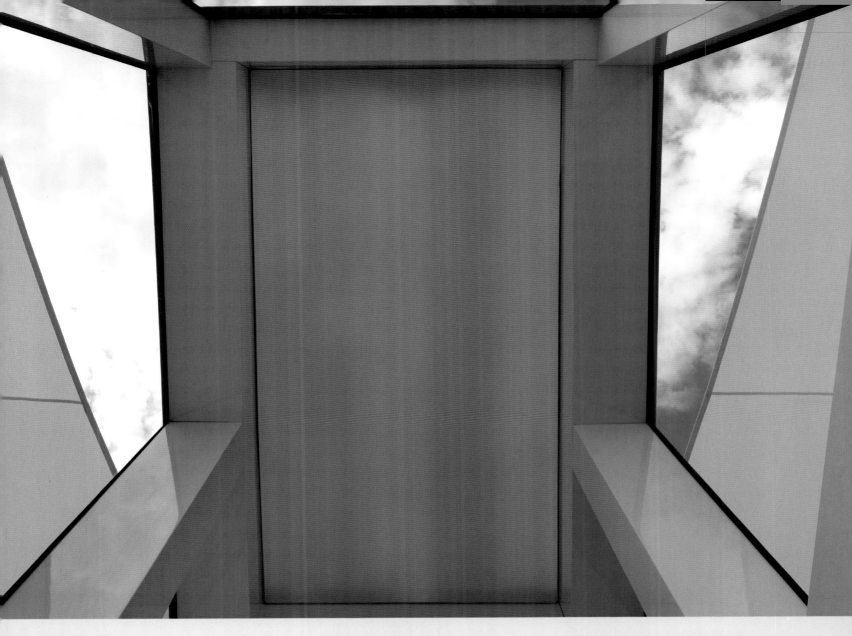

The upper deck saloon has a turret skylight. The turret roof can be opened and features LED lighting.

MASSIMO LISTRI

CASA MEDITERRANEA

SPECTACULAR HOUSES AND GLORIOUS GARDENS BY THE SEA

Text by Nicoletta del Buono

With 339 color illustrations

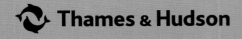

MEDITERRANEAN STYLE: A CONCEPTUAL GEOGRAPHY

Greece and Magna Graecia, Capri, the Amalfi Coast, Versilia and the Riviera, the Costa Smeralda, the Aeolian Islands, the Spanish Balearic Islands, Malta and the north African coastline. There is a common thread linking these places together. It is not just the sea that shimmers around them, or the radiant sunshine that envelops them. Nor is it the traces of ancient human activity which remind us that the sea has always been a watery highway for economic, political and cultural traffic.

They all have a special quality which the Italians call *Mediterraneità* but which we might describe as 'Mediterranean style' or 'Mediterranean essence'. It is an emotion, a state of mind that is born of centrality – a result of what the scholar of cultural phenomena, Alessandro Ubertazzi, called the mediation 'between the harshness of the poles and the abundance of the equator'. It is a place of the mind in which a wealth of accumulated thought can be disseminated to all. It is a state of being inextricably linked with humour and irony. 'Immediately north of the Alps', Ubertazzi observed, 'one encounters a traditional tendency to sarcasm and to the grotesque, while in countries even further north a desolation caused by lack of communication prevails, but around the 45° parallel, the Mediterranean line of latitude, people smile. If laughter is an external expression of simple high spirits, then smiling is symptomatic of a capacity for irony. Smiling is a typical expression of *Mediterraneità* and is perhaps an essential element in its recognition.'

This is reflected to the highest degree in Mediterranean architecture – in palaces, villas, houses, and even in the different ways the natural landscape has been tamed. For Le Corbusier, and for the pioneering Italian Rationalist Giuseppe Terragni, *Mediterraneità* symbolized the seed of classicism and was an antidote to the extreme geometric nature of Northern functionalism. This is demonstrated by vibrant contradictions of colour and volume, by exteriors that use the purest white and interiors that delight us with their powerful, primary colours, by the close proximity of simplicity and superabundance, and of the past and the present. It is defined by the boundary between 'interior' and 'exterior': the interior which, to quote Ubertazzi again, 'is a place for mediation, a place for intelligence, invention and exchanges, while the exterior is the *thesaurum*, the home of diversity.'

Here Massimo Listri takes us on a journey of discovery as he explores this fascinating and complex geography, which is as conceptual as it is concrete. He does so with the skill of a seasoned traveller, replacing his notebook with the art that best fits his purpose – photography. It is both as explorer and poet that he visits these dwellings and islands in search of the true features of *Mediterraneità*. He presents it through the shapes, colours and objects that his experienced eye has brought together. The result is a superbly elegant visual study of Mediterranean style.

Opposite Dolce & Gabbana's villa on Stromboli is a masterpiece of Mediterranean architecture, its purist forms and colours fusing with the surrounding landscape.

THE KALLITSANTSIS RESIDENCE

Left Artistic ceramics decorate the table.

Right The villa has views out to sea and the island of Spetses.

Magda and Dimitris Kallitsantsis's holiday home is in Porto Heli, in the Argolis Prefecture. It was Dimitris Kallitsantsis's development company that made Santiago Calatrava's fabulous design for the Olympic Stadium in Athens a reality. The villa, built some years ago, has been radically rethought and renovated by husband and wife. The interior is traditionally furnished, and is filled with works of art and strong colours. Madga Kallitsantsis says, 'We chose blue as our principal colour, which I think of as being very Greek as it evokes the colours of my country's sea and sky. And we also used white and red as they are the very essence of Mediterranean style.'

Left, above Crimson walls and a red-and-white checked floor create a playful contrast in the swimming pool changing room. The antique bench and shelf, which are both examples of the local traditional style, have been painted in a characteristic Greek cobalt blue.

Left, below On a marble and wrought-iron console table is a sculpture by Sophia Vari, wife of Fernando Botero.

Opposite The staircase leading to the kitchen has also been painted in a deep blue. Another sculpture by Sophia Vari sits on the balustrade, and ceramics from the 1960s are displayed in the wall niches.

Right, above The master bedroom. Above the headboard is a painting, *The Sea*, by the Greek artist Pavlo.

Right, below The guest apartment includes an office, lounge and veranda.

Opposite In the living room, a mixed-technique work, *Filled*, by Pavlo hangs above the sofa. To the left, above the door, is a wood and plaster sculpture, *Magda and the Dragon*, by Pavlo Samio, which was inspired by Greek mythology.

Overleaf The terrace has stunning sea views. The base of the large sofa is built into the wall.

MASTRO RAPHAËL

Interior design by Mario Arcangeli

Left A collection of corals is arranged on an antique urn.

Right The dining-room table is made from recycled old wooden planks. The antique bench has a quilted cushion covered in *Country & Sea* cotton from Mastro Raphaël. The chairs are from Arcarosa. The terracotta floor and the stove are original features.

Mario Arcangeli is president of the textile and furnishing companies Mastro Raphaël and Arcarosa, which belong to the Mastro Raphaël Group and are among the best representatives of Italian style. He has created this private space adjoining his Porto Cervo showroom. It has a rarefied and tranquil atmosphere, fostered by the spirit of the place and local artisanal knowledge, but tempered by a modern sensibility. It is also filled with many reminders of the Costa Smeralda's harsh and rugged nature.

In the living room, naturalistic
collections of shells and corals stand
out among the Arcarosa furniture and
the Mastro Raphaël fabrics.

Right, above Coral embroidery on cushions from Mastro Raphaël.

Right, below More corals are displayed above the sofa on the wall. The walls have been whitewashed in typical Sardinian style.

Above The original stove, and next to it a chair from Arcarosa.

Left Next to the living-room fireplace are two *Edward* sofas covered with *Keralis* fabric from Mastro Raphaël. The *Alabarda* lamp is also from Mastro Raphaël. The niches are adorned with curious and precious objects.

NICOLETTA MARAZZA'S APARTMENT

Interior design by Nicoletta Marazza

I n Ramatuelle, Basse Provence, the Milanese interior designer Nicoletta Marazza has designed a small apartment inspired by the sun-drenched atmosphere of the Midi and Greece, by their nature, history and culture, and by their lively and superstitious religious sensibility.

Above Greek-style cushions in Mediterranean colours.

Opposite In the kitchen, iron fruit and cake stands are laden with fruit, vegetables and shells to create unusual still lifes.

Above In the small Greek-style sitting room, aubergine-coloured mattresses have been used as sofas and adorned with multi-coloured cushions. The copper *Papiro* lamp is by Pallucco. The small panels on the walls were painted by the owner, who was inspired by votive images from the Greek Orthodox Church.

Opposite The linen cupboard contains blankets.

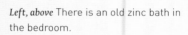

Left, above There is an old zinc bath in the bedroom.

Left, below An improvised washbasin with brass taps.

The bed in the master bedroom is hung with Provençal fabrics. The star-shaped lantern is Moroccan. The small wooden board above the mattress is a section of antique panelling.

Sorrento, Italy

LA MINERVETTA

Interior design by Marco De Luca

Left Two nineteenth-century gouaches depict Mount Vesuvius erupting.

Right A nineteenth-century side table displays old pieces of pottery, corals and sea urchins collected by the owner.

The Mediterranean, with its radiant light and its sunny, drama-filled culture, is the common thread of La Minervetta's diverse decor. This small, charming travellers' hideaway is much more than a hotel; it's a real home-from-home on the Sorrento Peninsula. The furniture, art objects, collections, materials, colour palette, and the sophisticated references it contains have all been orchestrated with a theatrical sensibility designed to emphasize the incomparable beauty of its panoramic views of the sea.

Overleaf The company Vietri Scotto, based in Vietri sul Mare, produced the maiolica tiles that cover the living-room floor. Books, model ships, and Solimene ceramic pieces from the 1960s have been combined with vases by Ettore Sottsass. The door to the kitchen is framed by two Baroque decorations made from cardboard which were once used in religious processions.

Opposite and above The kitchen is a true architectural gem where guests can eat breakfast and sample the homemade jam. The walls are covered with maiolica tiles from Vietri.

The relaxation area has sea views.

Above The port of Sorrento.

Left The staircase has been carved out of the rock.

Above (left) Double bed with a tall
coral-red headboard; (right) Detail
of a wardrobe with coral-shaped
handles, designed by Marco De Luca.

Opposite A bathroom counter top and
lower wall decorated with striped
maiolica tiles from Vietri.

Overleaf The swimming pool overlooks
the sea.

DOLCE & GABBANA'S VILLA

The building's pure white exterior breaks the continuity of the deep blue sea and the sky. Its purist forms, facing onto the sweet-scented, harsh, lava-strewn landscape, rise and fall to absorb the stresses of the volcanic earth. This is the initial impression of Domenico Dolce and Stefano Gabbana's villa in Piscità on the island of Stromboli. Inside, however, the stark white of the exterior gives way to an eclectic explosion of colour, a profusion of objects, decorative curios and ethnic artefacts. As in their fashion designs, D&G use the basic elements here too as a mocking Trojan horse for their vibrantly creative exuberance.

Right The patio is overlooked by the various sections of the villa. The towering peak of the volcano rises behind it.

Above Small traditional votive pictures hang in the blue room.

Right The blue room is decorated with a row of Sicilian dolls hanging from the exposed beams of the ceiling. Caltagirone tiles cover the floor.

Overleaf Domenico Dolce's green bedroom. The Sicilian furniture dates from the early twentieth century.

Kitchen with dining area. The two
designers chose to cover the walls
with innumerable Caltagirone ceramic
fragments in an overwhelming but
charming display of pattern and colour.
The ceramic heads on the structure
above the door were also made in
Caltagirone's kilns.

Right, above The walls and floor of the dining room have also been painstakingly covered with a virtual mosaic of Caltagirone ceramics.

Right, below In this corner of the kitchen, which is used for preparing ingredients, the niche contains numerous pieces of crockery from Calatino in Sicily.

53

The two designers adore the sunny
colour of the yellow bedroom. Two
ironic portraits of Dolce and Gabbana,
depicted respectively as San Domenico
(on the right) and Santo Stefano,
hang on the wall. The bed is covered
in leopard-print fabric, as are the
nineteenth-century armchairs.

Left The spaces between the buildings include natural elements such as this olive tree. The landscape has become a discreet and poetic part of the domestic setting.

Opposite A detail of the terrace by the sea. The zebra-striped fabrics are a reminder of Dolce and Gabbana's passion for animal prints.

Above and opposite From some angles the
villa resembles a citadel. Its whiteness
and purist forms are the dominant
elements, contrasting powerfully with
the deep pellucid blues of the sea and
the sky, and with the plastic shapes
made by nature which has gradually
infiltrated the architecture.

Overleaf View of the villa from the west.
The pure white of the architecture
stands out sharply against the black
volcanic rock.

VILLA SAN MICHELE

Villa San Michele perches on a hillside north-east of Anacapri. It is 327 metres (1,073 feet) above sea level and boasts views across sapphire-blue waters towards the Gulf of Naples. Designed by Axel Munthe as his own home, today it houses a museum of the numerous archaeological finds acquired by the Swedish physician during the many years that he lived on the island of Capri. Munthe's experiences are wonderfully retold in his book, *The Story of San Michele*. Built around the turn of the twentieth century on the ruins of an imperial Roman villa – some traces of which are still visible in the garden – the villa's architecture is a blend of the fantastic and the bizarre, which mirrors the eclectic and historicist symbolism that pervades its internal decoration and the taste that informs its collections.

Above Villa San Michele is situated 327 metres above sea level. To reach it, one must climb the 777 Phoenician Steps which lead from Capri town to Anacapri.

Opposite The villa's Egyptian sphinx.

Right A view of the sculpture gallery.

Opposite The sculpture gallery contains a thirteenth-century marble slab decorated with Cosmati mosaics which may once have adorned the altar of a convent. Axel Munthe found it in a little village not far from Palermo, where it was being used as a laundry board. Five miniature columns with capitals have been placed beneath the slab. The museum contains 1,650 finds, many of which are of Etruscan and Roman origin.

Left In the small study a stone Medusa head, which Munthe claimed to have discovered at the bottom of the sea, stands out above the writing desk.

Opposite Archaeological finds in the atrium of the villa. The loggia can be seen in the background, and a copy of a female statue from Herculaneum is set in a niche.

Li Galli, Italy

GIOVANNI RUSSO'S HOUSE

Gallo Lungo, Castelluccio and La Rotonda are three tiny islands which make up the archipelago of Li Galli off the Amalfi Coast. The choreographer and Russian ballet dancer Léonide Massine bought the three islands in 1924 and built a villa on the largest island, Gallo Lungo, on the site of Roman ruins. The property was expanded some years later with a series of additions by Le Corbusier, and with a guest annex. In 1989 the world-renowned ballet dancer Rudolf Nureyev took over ownership from Massine, and when Nureyev died in 1993 the archipelago was acquired by Giovanni Russo, a talented entrepreneur and leading figure in today's cultural scene. Russo has retained most of Nureyev's renovations to the villa and the nearby Saracen tower, and today it is still possible to enjoy the eclectic, cosmopolitan, exuberant and, above all, nautical air which the great dancer bestowed upon it.

Above The archipelago of Li Galli lies near the coast of Positano. On the largest of its three islands, Gallo Lungo, are a thirteenth-century Saracen tower, a large villa, an annex and an adjoining chapel.

Right The Saracen tower in which Rudolf Nureyev created four floors with nine bedrooms, five bathrooms and a gymnasium. A relic of the era in which pirates sailed the Tyrrhenian Sea, it was Nureyev's favourite hideaway and he loved to spend his vacations here in the company of his closest friends, including Franco Zeffirelli and Vittoria Ottolenghi.

Left, above The living room in the tower. The large windows have a view of the barely tamed nature on Gallo Lungo. The border of antique ceramic Vietri tiles was made by Nureyev. Search lights, telescopes and a model ship give the room a nautical feel.

Left, below Detail of the villa's dining room. Two ancient Greek vases stand on the nineteenth-century marquetry table from Sorrento.

Opposite The kitchen stonework is in the style of *opus incertum* (a Roman construction technique using irregular stones) and painted white.

The music room typifies the villa. The cushions are from Mastro Raphaël, the table-bench decorated with cockerels is African, and the hi-fi system is from Bang & Olufsen. The walls are covered in antique ceramic tiles chosen by Nureyev, who loved mosaic patterns.

Above The main bathroom.

Opposite The coral motif, a favourite element of Amalfi traditional handicrafts, is also used in the sleeping area of the annex. Greta Garbo, Roberto Rossellini, Anna Magnani, Ingrid Bergman, Jacqueline Kennedy and Aristotle Onassis and, more recently, Hillary Clinton have been among the many famous visitors to Li Galli.

An individual mood has been created for each of these two bedrooms. The first (above), in the tower, is inspired by the Orient, emphasized by the collection of objects on the shelves and table. The second (opposite), in the main villa, draws inspiration from the Arab world in the colours of the wardrobe and the geometric wall decoration.

Overleaf In the villa's master bedroom, the balcony doorway frames an unrivalled vista of a limitless sea. The marine theme is continued in the interior by an array of undersea creatures, displayed on shelves which also function as room dividers.

Above Detail of the villa exterior.

Left Nestling between the rocks of the island, the spectacular swimming pool seems to merge with the sea and almost to touch the island of Castelluccio.

Marrakesh, Morocco

MINISTERO DEL GUSTO

Interior design by Alessandra Lippini and Fabrizio Bizzarri

Left The exterior walls of the Ministero del Gusto are painted a deep ochre colour. The windows that open onto the terrace have corrugated iron shutters.

Right The roof terrace functions as an open-air lounge.

Ministero del Gusto, the most innovative gallery-studio in Marrakesh, is tucked away down a little alleyway in the Medina. Quite unlike any Western gallery and highly unconventional, it is arranged like a house but has the air of an imaginary oriental palace. Visitors wind their way through showrooms which are enlivened by strangely shaped fireplaces, ethnic artefacts and objects created from natural materials. The rooms thus become more than open spaces to display artworks and superb handicrafts. Works by the French painter François Lelong and the Moroccan artist Hassan Hajjaj stand out, as do the unique pieces by Alessandra Lippini and Fabrizio Bizzarri who love to combine modern and ethnic elements.

Above, left The balcony of the inner
courtyard has a richly decorated
parapet.

Above, right Inner courtyard. In the
foreground is a sculpture by François
Lelong. In front of the pool are several
mortars carved from the trunks of
mangrove trees. Wooden poles are
suspended above the pool and serve
as a focal point.

Opposite The balustrade of the
staircase is made of rope from
fishermen's nets.

Left, above A wall densely covered with hieroglyphic decoration.

Left, below A bathroom.

Opposite One of the rooms draws from nature, with small zebra-striped armchairs and collections of tree branches and antlers. The ceiling is painted with natural pigments.

Overleaf A Lounge Chair by Charles Eames (in the foreground) is displayed with furniture by Lippini and Bizzarri.

Porto Cervo, Italy

CASA STARAK

Interior design by Patrice Nourissat

Parisian interior designer Patrice Nourissat has redefined this house on the Costa Smeralda primarily through the use of strong Mediterranean colours, which act as catalysts of energy. Cobalt blue, fuchsia pink and flaming orange create a powerful contrast with the neutral shades of Sardinian granite. Elements from different cultures, from the East and from Africa, are combined here. The furniture was made by Sardinian and Polish craftsmen and complements the Berber fabrics and Indonesian decorative objects perfectly in a happy synthesis.

Above The dining room resembles a grotto carved out of the granite rock, highlighting another key theme of the house – nature and architecture in harmony.

Opposite Cobalt blue arches give rhythm to the corridor. The stone bust is by Anna Malicka Zamorska.

Left View of the dining room, with a stone Khmer sculpture.

Opposite The iron four-poster bed has been draped with orange voiles. An exotic air enlivens this African room.

Left The living room is characterized by the intense orange colour of its walls. The straw chair-sculpture at the foot of the steps is by the Polish designer Pawel Grunert. The CD player is from Bang & Olufsen.

Overleaf The blue pool floor intensifies the reflections in the water.

THE ETRO RESIDENCE

Designed by Emilio Carcano

Left The entrance. Beside
a Gothic-style column is a
fragment of marble sculpture.

Right The crenellated tower and
the terrace on the top floor of
the palace.

A fifteenth-century palace nestling between
Roman walls overlooks the Arab market and
the port of Dalt Vila in Ibiza, its crenellated tower
contrasting sharply with the intense blue of the sky
and the sea. Gimmo and Roberta Etro fell in love
with it, bought it and breathed new life into it with
the help of architect Emilio Carcano, long-time
collaborator of the set designer Renzo Mongiardino.
Carcano's meticulous restoration, while preserving
the exterior intact, has liberated the palace from
the accretions that were suffocating it, bringing
light and air to its interior spaces. Roberta Etro
took charge of the interior decoration, which now
mirrors its owners' culture and character.

Beside the fireplace in the reception room is a Gandhara statue of a warrior. It is carved from schist stone and dates from the sixteenth century.

Above The terrace has a canopied dining area.

Left An open-air living room has been created on the terrace.

Saint-Tropez, France

FRÉDÉRIC MECHICHE'S HOUSE

Designed by Frédéric Mechiche

In a seventeenth-century building in the La Ponche district of Saint-Tropez, where the traditional charm of the Midi is still preserved intact, the French architect Frédéric Mechiche wanted to accentuate the simplicity of the rooms with their high ceilings and pervasive Mediterranean light by using strong colour contrasts. Black brushstrokes stand out against the pure white of the walls and sofas, and there are sudden unexpected touches of acid green. Over time, the space had become filled with unnecessary partitions and lowered ceilings. Mechiche has rescued the original well-proportioned spaces, opened up doors and vaulted passageways, restored the ancient terracotta floors, softened period architectural detailing and introduced important contemporary artworks.

Left In the kitchen, graphic works in black and white contrast with the acid-green walls.

Right The living room. Above the French Regency fireplace, its whitewashed surround stripped of all surplus decoration, is a wall drawing by Sol LeWitt. The sofas and tables were designed by Mechiche. The *Glo-Ball* floor lamp is a Jasper Morrison design for Flos, and a work by Andres Serrano hangs on the wall behind it. The original Provençal flooring has been finished with white resin.

The TV room is lit by lamps from Flos. The door is a trompe l'œil illusion; on the wall beside it hangs a work by Andy Warhol depicting James Dean. On the wall to the left is *Ejaculation in trajectory* by Andres Serrano from 1989. The suspended sculpture is by Ernesto Neto.

Right, above On the walls of the corridor are prints of poetry by Carl Andre.

Right, below A wall drawing by Sol LeWitt.

In the living room are works in iron by
Sophie Calle. The wool-covered chairs
date from the 1940s and came from
Christian Dior's atelier. The lamps are
from Flos.

The kitchen walls are painted acid-green. On the left are instructions for wall drawings by Sol LeWitt. The series of abstract monochromes on the right is by Caillere. The steel-fronted cupboards have white Carrara marble tops. The chandelier is by Swarovski.

The master bedroom. The bed was
designed by Mechiche. The small
green resin chair is a prototype by
Chris Grattan. In the background, a
column lamp is set into a long niche
in the wall. The pendant lamp on the
right dates from the 1960s.

ROBERTO MANCINI'S HOUSE

Interior design by Marianna Gagliardi

This house on the Costa Smeralda belongs to a true gentleman of Italian football, Roberto Mancini, and reflects his tastes, his love of art and antiques, but also the importance of privacy to him. It is a haven for family and friends. Redesigned by Marianna Gagliardi, who was careful to preserve the solid granite of the walls and door frames, the house combines vibrant shades of white and sky-blue with Mediterranean touches, drawing inspiration from Provençal and Greek decorative styles, and from nature. Mancini's wife is particularly passionate about shells, which are a prominent feature of the decor.

Right The veranda is a perfect extension of the reception room. The sofa was made especially for the space. A French nineteenth-century wire plant-holder adorns the pillar.

Left The dining room. The table is French and dates from the early twentieth century. The shell painting on silk is by Eric Peyret.

Opposite Another of Peyret's shell works dominates the living room. The side table in the foreground and the lamp with ceramic base are also French and date from the nineteenth century.

Above A specially designed sofa and wicker armchair create an intimate relaxation area by the pool.

Opposite View at night of the deck-level swimming pool which features LED lighting.

Pantelleria, Italy

ANGELA PINTALDI'S HOUSE

Interior design by Angela Pintaldi

Angela Pintaldi is a dynamic and passionate Sicilian, and a mercurial designer of unique and opulent jewelry made from semi-precious stones and natural materials. She has created a hideaway that reflects her character on the island of Pantelleria, in a rugged and austere *dammuso* which she has crammed with ethnic objects from countries such as Tibet, India and Morocco. *Dammusi* are the characteristic, ancient buildings of Pantelleria. Their dry-stone walls are made with blocks of volcanic rock.

Right Exterior view. The *dammuso* is situated in the valley of Monastero, and opens onto the side of Montagna Grande mountain, which dominates the island.

The interior of the *dammuso* is a single
large room articulated by arches and
vaults. The carved wooden four-
poster bed once belonged to an Indian
princess, and its curtains are, in fact,
antique saris. The cushions are covered
with Berber fabrics. In the foreground
are Indian glasses and Moroccan
storage jars.

Right, above Antique Indian furniture beside a small window.

Right, below Antique Tibetan furniture, and rugs from the same region. On the floor are lacquered Chinese boxes.

Left The border above the washbasin was designed by Angela Pintaldi using fragments of Sicilian pots. The antique silver candleholders are from India.

Opposite Out in the open and protected by the walls, jasmine thrives in antique Greek amphorae. Traditional Sicilian ceramic plates are arranged on an Indian chest.

VILLA OLIVETTA

Designed by David Chipperfield
Interior design by Giorgio Fornari and Ferruccio Laviani

Stefano Gabbana's Villa Olivetta in Portofino is part of a complex of four buildings – which also includes Domenico Dolce's Villa Bianca and the guest villas La Vigna and Cisterna – purchased by the designers Dolce and Gabbana and redesigned by the English architect David Chipperfield. While Dolce opted for a fairy-tale white throughout his villa, the more romantic and bohemian Gabbana chose a different theme for each room of his Villa Olivetta, which has a castle-like turret. He has not taken his inspiration from one single Mediterranean source, but has created an exotic rhapsody of nautical and tropical motifs.

Right A detail of the dining room. The walls and floor are decorated with a fantastic patchwork of fragments of mirrors and Sicilian pottery.

Opposite This terrace has a swimming pool which is only used during the summer months. In winter it is hidden from view beneath the terrace and covered over with large stone slabs.

Overleaf The fantastical Hawaiian decoration on the walls is by the artist Michael Lin. The table, designed by Ferruccio Laviani, complements the Louis XV-style chairs. The rug is from the 1960s.

Above A detail of the mosaic floor, made from irregular pottery fragments, in the dining room.

Left A curious assortment of coloured glass lanterns light the dining room.

The trompe l'œil ceiling in a guest
bedroom continues the zebra-stripe
theme of the carpeting.

The lounge is illuminated by Swarovski crystal chandeliers. Works by Marc Chagall, Lucio Fontana and Andy Warhol hang on the walls.

135

A chinchilla-fur bedspread and tiger-
skin rug adorn the master bedroom.

Right, above The white Corian bath seems to float like an iceberg on the dark wenge floor.

Right, below The large mirror with a gilded frame in the master bedroom is nineteenth century.

Above The marble spiral staircase has been covered over with stained teak panelling as part of Chipperfield's design. The neon installation *Love* is by Ferruccio Laviani.

Left Red and gold silk brocade covers the walls of a guest bedroom, which contains Chinoiserie furniture.

Overleaf In the living room, a large curving sofa by Laviani has ocelot upholstery.

139

Gudja, Malta

VILLA DORELL

Left A view of the garden from the sixteenth-century tower of the palace.

Right Another view of the garden, which features ornate stone sculptures of animals and plants. The sixteenth-century tower can be seen on the right.

This Baroque palace, also known as the Palazzo d'Aurel, sits in Malta's well-manicured countryside not far from the village of Gudja. It is intimately linked with the history of the island, in particular with the story of Bettina Dorell, a lady companion to Maria Carolina of Austria, Queen of the Kingdom of the Two Sicilies, and wife of Diego Moscati Sceberras, Marquis of Xrobb-il-Ghagin, a powerful Maltese aristocrat who became embroiled in a notorious anti-Masonic trial. In the second half of the eighteenth century, it was she who commissioned the extravagantly landscaped garden and oversaw the exuberant decoration of the interiors, which hover between the Baroque and the Neoclassical.

Above A prayer corner from a sixteenth-century hermit's refuge has been placed in the garden.

Opposite A hallway in the residence. The trompe l'œil and torch-holder lend a fairy-tale atmosphere.

A view of the palace at night from an avenue in the park.

Forte dei Marmi, Italy

VILLA VIRGINIA

Interior design by Nicola Falcone
Garden by Giuseppe Martini

Left The entrance portico has a floor of pink Trani stone. In the foreground are two African sculptures, originally from Mali. The fountain was made from a design by the owner.

Right The portico overlooks the swimming pool, which has a glass mosaic bottom and is edged with Ipe wood boards. The garden was designed by Giuseppe Martini.

Nicola Falcone's fantastic designs have turned the interior of this neo-Rationalist villa, hidden among the pinewoods of Forte dei Marmi, into a treasure chest of nautical themes. Elliptical plasterboard structures on the ceiling create a ripple effect through the living room, and sliding panels decorated with an image of gigantic fronds of seaweed separate the living room from the kitchen. The house is suffused with the colours of waves, shells and corals.

Above A corner of the living room, with the *Corralich* console table designed by Nicola Falcone and a painting by Paolo Emilio Gironda.

Right The living room. Plasterboard ellipses attached to the ceiling and sliding panels with a seaweed design (a work by Ludwig Hartmann) give the room a definite nautical mood. The mirror-sculpture *Ring*, on the right, is by Falcone. The sofa is from Edra, and the dining table is from Avallone. *Mater Baby*, another piece by Hartmann, hangs on the wall to the left.

Left The bedroom. On the left is *Boy One* by Ludwig Hartmann, a graphic reworking of a graffiti piece. The picture on the right is by Paolo Emilio Gironda. The iron and ostrich-skin bedside tables with crystal balls were designed and made by Nicola Falcone.

Right One corner of the bedroom. The *Marina* console table in nickel-plated iron is by Falcone, and the leather rug was inlaid and studded by Falcone and Hartmann.

Overleaf The villa and the swimming pool at night.

Marrakesh, Morocco

BERBER FORTRESS

Left The stone gateway of the former fortress.

Right The terraced roof of the kasbah. The walls, made from a mixture of mud and straw, have been treated with quicklime and painted with natural pigments.

In Talamanzou, French art expert Jean-Yves Barczyk has created his hideaway from the world: a Berber fortress built on the ruins of a nineteenth-century kasbah. He has restored the fortress, preserving both the old mud and straw walls, so typical of local building traditions, and the windows with deflectors which ventilate the rooms. He has filled the interior with exquisitely tasteful oriental furniture and art objects.

Left, above The entrance corridor. The large carved wooden door came from a nineteenth-century granary. The zouak chest has pyroengraved decoration.

Left, below The entrance hall. A collection of Berber terracotta pots is arranged on the locally made wooden shelving.

Opposite Antique Berber rugs make the reception room warm and welcoming.

Overleaf The hanging lamps and brass tables in the lounge were found in a Marrakesh souk.

Pages 162–163 Berber pots on the roof.

Ibiza, Spain

CAN MIGUEL TONI IN SAN CARLOS

Designed by Ralph Blackstad
Garden by Sandy Pratt

In Ibiza, an ancient *finca* (farmhouse) belonging to an internationally renowned art collector has been renovated by the Canadian architect Ralph Blackstad. He has emphasized the original design, salvaged local materials such as stone and seasoned wood, and used colours typical of the island. The designer Sandy Pratt worked on the garden and introduced rare trees and luxuriant tropical flowers to grow among the native aromatic shrubs. The result is a Mediterranean symphony of exotic meanderings.

Right The exterior of the *finca*. The pure white of the walls stands out against the lush vegetation.

Above A seventeenth-century Italian
table and chairs are in the dining room.
The prints on the wall are nineteenth
century. The stand in the foreground, to
the right, has been piled high with straw
hats.

Opposite A Caucasian rug adds warmth
to the living room. A selection of antique
Indonesian, Indian and Afghan musical
instruments stands out against the
walls. The pouf and the cushions on the
sofa are covered with Caucasian fabrics.

A view of the living room from the entrance hall. The whitewashed walls are in stark contrast to the dark ceiling beams, which come from native Balearic Island savin trees. The two chairs are Spanish, and the floor is covered with rough terracotta tiles.

Above A sofa covered in Indian fabrics is perfect for relaxing in the arcaded loggia.

Left A pergola at the far end of the swimming pool contains a large swing seat which functions as a double bed.

CASA BORGOGNI

Interior design by Paolo Ignesti

Left The white Carrara marble staircase is original to the house and has been moved to create a mezzanine.

Right The kitchen has a black slate floor and a glass wall facing onto the garden. The grille protecting the glass has cast-iron columns that came from the old railway station in Pistoia. The unusual stove is French, as is the seventeenth-century cast-iron griffon plant stand. The white marble washbasin came from an old Genoese fishermen's cottage. The oval flower painting is nineteenth-century Italian.

In Pietrasanta in the Versilian hinterland, architect Paolo Ignesti has remodelled a small early twentieth-century villa, giving it a much more modern mood without neglecting its Mediterranean roots. On the contrary, he has emphasized this aspect by using sunny colours which help to define the different rooms and their functions, and by using materials and objects that are of local or French origin.

Above A corner of the living/dining room.
The bench is early twentieth century.
The French plant stand dates from the
seventeenth century.

Left The blue lounge. The walls have
been painted in Tunisian blue. The
beautiful floor is original.

Above, left The Autumn Room is painted in shades of ochre and orange. The sofa conceals a bed.

Above, right The Winter Room is furnished with early twentieth-century German furniture.

Opposite A detail of the Autumn Room with the original floor.

COLONNA DI POMPEO, OBELISCO DI CLEOPATRA

The washbasins in the bathroom
adjoining the Spring Room are made
from Florentine breccia.

Elba, Italy

CASA CATASTINI

Designed by Marianna Gagliardi
Garden by Pietro Porcinai

The island of Elba embodies the true essence of the Tyrrhenian Sea. Here, architect Marianna Gagliardi has remodelled a villa by rediscovering the local proportions and the deep roots of Mediterranean myth, even when it has been filtered by British colonial culture. The house, built originally in the 1950s, has been reinterpreted in a contemporary way. Its teak floors give it the air of an enormous clipper ship on the high seas, and it is filled with pieces of antique furniture, traditional Tuscan, Indian and colonial decorative objects and materials, as well as modern works of art. The ship-like villa is thus freighted with references to different cultures and to different ways of living with the sea.

Left The Tyrrhenian Sea glimpsed through an arched window in the arcade.

Opposite Plumbago and bougainvillea bushes scramble over the pillars of the arcade. The sofa and armchairs are made of wicker.

Overleaf The swimming pool with a view of the sea.

Above The dining room, where three nineteenth-century cherry wood tables have been pushed together to create one large surface.

Opposite The kitchen/dining space has an impressive beamed ceiling.

Overleaf The large living room looks out over the swimming pool. Both the model sailing ship and the Aubusson carpet are nineteenth century. The original beams have been painted sky-blue.

The entrance space has been transformed into a winter garden with the addition of a glass roof. The painted wooden bench (left) is seventeenth century.

RIDUM DE PIRO

Designed by Noel Debattista

The rural estate Ridum de Piro, built in a typical Maltese style that unites Greek and British architectural traditions, was purchased by Englishman Jeffrey Mizzi and redesigned by the architect Noel Debattista, who has retained its dual Eastern and Anglo-Saxon nature with meticulous care. The furniture was sourced from the Cyclades and Provence, while the colours were drawn from a Mediterranean palette.

Right The house built out of the ancient estate overlooks a large deck-level swimming pool which almost seems to continue on into the sea. Some of the farm buildings are more than four centuries old.

Left The fireplace in the master bedroom.

Opposite The guest bedroom with its nineteenth-century wrought-iron four-poster bed.

Overleaf A hammock suspended between two olive trees is a reminder that the garden is intended to be a space for relaxation.

Port Lligat, Spain

SALVADOR DALÍ'S HOUSE

In the 1930s Salvador Dalí and his wife Gala transformed a simple fishermen's cottage in Port Lligat into a retreat from the world, somewhere to escape to during the long summer months. They enlarged it and added new buildings, always mindful of the natural differences in height in the rocky ground. The Fundació Gala-Salvador Dalí carried out meticulous restoration work on the house, which today is open to the public. It appears as a complex conglomeration of articulated and dislocated structures spread out over different levels with its patios, white walls, local stones and materials, precious relics and references to classical mythology. It is also a fascinating insight into the celebrated Catalan artist – an exuberant synthesis of references to a red-blooded and eclectic Mediterranean style that came more from the heart than the location.

Left Two large heads representing Castor and Pollux dominate the boundary wall of the complex. Dalí saw parallels between this myth and his own relationship with Gala.

Opposite Next to the olive grove, the pigeon loft is surmounted by gigantic white eggs, which are symbols of life.

Above the shelves and cupboards are
stuffed animals and fragrant local herbs
hung up to dry.

The walls of the dressing room are covered with photographs and magazine covers with references to Dalí. This collection could almost be seen as a chronicle of the artist's life and times.

Left Dalí and Gala's bedroom can be glimpsed beyond the fireplace. The beds have a draped canopy surmounted with an imperial eagle. The steps and the floor are covered with thick-textured matting.

Opposite A staircase leads to the dressing room for the models who posed for Dalí. On the wall is an enlarged photograph of a sea urchin, and a giant oriental umbrella dominates the entire scene.

Above In the garden is a copy of the
fountain from the Patio de los Leones
which adorns the Alhambra in Granada.

Right Dalí's house overlooks the bay of
Port Lligat. The island of Farnera can be
seen in the distance.

Tellaro, Italy

CASA MASCOTTO

Designed by Tiziano Lera

This converted watchtower, on a promontory overlooking the Gulf of Poets in north-west Italy, is in subtle harmony with the sea and sunshine. Tiziano Lera, with the assistance of Ignazio Ferrari, consolidated the structure without making any substantial modifications and preserved the building's original irregularity. Shells appear throughout the building, along with bronze octopus sculptures and paintings which evoke the sea and the natural world. Mediterranean colours have also been used in all of the rooms.

Above Three large shells are arranged on the window sill of the fourth-floor living room which has sea views.

Opposite The house has been created from a tower which was once used to look out for pirate ships.

Above, left The staircase leading to the upper floors.

Above, right The bronze fireplace with octopus sculptures. According to local tradition, this creature brings good luck.

Opposite Beside the sofa in the living room stands a nineteenth-century model of a sailing ship.

Right The roof garden.

Opposite Breakfast is served on the terrace. The lamp with octopus detail is an original work by Tiziano Lera.

CLAUDIO BRAVO'S HOUSE

Chilean painter Claudio Bravo's home in Tangier is a compendium of ancient, modern and contemporary art. It is an oasis of peace, a Mediterranean fantasy, and a link between East and West. Just a kilometre from the kasbah, it was built in the early nineteenth century for a political advisor in Tangier. It has now been renovated and transformed, and is a modernized version of the traditional Moroccan style, or rather of the local colonial style. Its columns, arches, whitewashed walls and patios all bear witness to the Portuguese, Spanish and English cultures which have ruled over Tangier. This is all combined with ancient and contemporary sculpture, and design classics.

Right A view of the house from the Mediterranean garden, which is filled with palm trees and eucalyptus. A portico supported by columns runs along the front of the building.

Above The artist's studio is divided
into seven rooms. Its arched windows
directly look out to sea. A glass-topped
table by Mies van der Rohe, displaying
an Italian bronze of a horse, can be
glimpsed in the lounge area to the right.

Opposite Beyond an arch of the portico
is the garden, planted with hydrangeas
and different varieties of palm trees.

Above In the living room, a self-portrait
by Claudio Bravo hangs above the
sofa. The chair came from Tétouan in
northern Morocco.

Right The little armchairs in the dining
room are Moroccan, as is the hanging
lantern above the table. There are some
ancient sculpture fragments on the
console table by the windows.

Left, above Alternate round and Moorish arches are a feature of the covered walkway on the upper floor. The base of the parapet is covered in mosaic.

Left, below A view of the lounge. The doorway is framed by two narwhal tusks.

The master bedroom has a wrought-iron four-poster bed. By the window, next to a Moroccan side table, is the famous Chaise Longue in pony skin by Le Corbusier, Pierre Jeanneret and Charlotte Perriand. The lantern is Moroccan.

Forte dei Marmi, Italy

ERMANNO SCERVINO'S HOUSE

Interior design by Ermanno Scervino

Left A lounge area by the kitchen. A plaster marlin and two necklaces from the Philippines are on the wall.

Right The living room. A shield from New Guinea hangs above the Louis XIV console table. A portrait of the actress Olivia de Havilland is inscribed to Ermanno Scervino, and a Marilyn Monroe screen print by Andy Warhol can be glimpsed below the console. On the wall to the right is a collection of plaster casts of Roman coins.

In the heart of Forte dei Marmi, the designer Ermanno Scervino has created a perfect retreat with a garden, far from the madding crowd. This is a house where time stands still and it is filled with influences absorbed from local tradition. It evokes childhood, carefree holidays, escape, memories, evenings at the Capannina club and literary recollections. This is a house where the sea exists as an idea, rather than as a physical presence.

A view of the kitchen from the entrance
hall. The photographs of Marilyn Monroe
are originals. In the background are two
portraits of Mao Zedong by Andy Warhol.

Above In the living room, a portrait of Andy Warhol hangs above a nineteenth-century French armchair. In the 1980s, Scervino was associated with The Factory, Warhol's famous New York studio.

Overleaf The living-room fireplace. A small collection of crabs carved from bone is displayed on the mantelpiece.

Right A bedroom with a Biedermeier bed.

Opposite In the master bedroom, the painting *Shin-On* by Shuhei Matsuyama stands out above the wicker bed. A Biedermeier table is used as a bedside table and displays a porcelain Portuguese vase.

Tangier, Morocco

AICHA BENHIMA'S HOUSE

Designed by Stewart Church

In northern Morocco, not far from Tétouan, the American architect Stewart Church has created a summer residence perched above the sea for Aicha Benhima and her family. It is inspired by Aicha's eclectic and curious background; she is a lady-in-waiting to Princess Lalla Meryem and a woman of a thousand interests. Church has given a modern twist to typical stylistic features of Islamic-Maghribi architecture and combined them with Andalusian, Indian and colonial decorative elements.

Right The bottom of the star-shaped deck-level swimming pool is covered with a material that increases the water's reflective properties. A small octagonal pavilion is positioned at the very edge of the garden overlooking the sea to catch the salt-laden breezes.

Overleaf The Moroccan lounge has painted doors which imitate models from the past. The walls have been treated with tadelakt lime plaster.

Above The façade of the villa facing the
sea. The windows of the winter garden
can be seen on the ground floor, and the
balcony of the master bedroom is on the
first floor.

Opposite The pavilion overlooking the sea
is at the bottom of the garden.

Above Another lounge. A silver tray rests on a Moroccan side table.

Opposite Another view of the Moroccan lounge. The terracotta floor is embellished with inlay of small ceramic tiles. The arch was inspired by traditional Indian Mughal style.

Right An intimate dining area in the winter garden. The chairs were designed by Stewart Church.

Opposite The wonderful view from the window makes this the perfect place to take breakfast.

Cattolica, Italy

ALBERTA FERRETTI'S HOUSE

Interior design by Alberta Ferretti

The designer Alberta Ferretti has found her lost paradise in a nineteenth-century villa that she first discovered as a child in Cattolica, in Emilia Romagna. It is her holiday home and a home for her memories, the realization of a dream. She has spent three years carefully restoring it, working on it as if it were one of her own dresses, and filling it with the finest fabrics, with oriental and Empire-style furniture, Venetian chandeliers, and modern and contemporary works of art.

Left In a corner of the living room is an eighteenth-century Japanese vase and an English 'magic' candle lamp.

Opposite On the terrace overlooking the sea is a late nineteenth-century elm wood Chinese stool.

Above The living-room fireplace. Above the fireplace is a painting by Kris Rush. The matelassé sofa was designed by Alberta Ferretti. A Chinese Kuang Hsu side table made from elm wood and rattan is in the foreground.

Left In the entrance hall is a late nineteenth-century Genoese table. Two *spolveri* (charcoal dust pounced through holes) by Adolfo de Carolis hang on the wall. On the floor are two Moroccan lanterns.

Left, above The dining room features a late nineteenth-century French chandelier. Chinese Kuang Hsu chairs are arranged around the table.

Left, below Another corner of the living room. The table is French, while the chair is Chinese.

Opposite A glass table is laid in the orangery, where the designer loves to host informal dinners. The silver nickel chairs are Indian.

Right A swing seat, designed by Alberta Ferretti, is draped with an Indian bedspread embroidered with silver thread.

Opposite On the terrace is a daybed, also designed by Ferretti. The rug and lamps are Moroccan.

Overleaf Beside the antique Indian frames are two lamps with shell diffusers, designed by Ferretti. The stools are African.

CASA BONAMIGO

On the Costa Smeralda, a holiday home immersed in greenery and overlooking the Baia del Pevero brings ethnic elements together with Mediterranean materials and handicrafts. The owner, Mariangela Bonamigo, adores colour which is the dominant feature of the house, often drawing inspiration from Tricia Guild's lively fabric designs.

Left The poufs and the ethnic lantern on the terrace are of African origin.

Opposite An alfresco dining area has been created on the upper terrace.

Above A corner of the living room.
The curtains are from Designers Guild.

Left The master bedroom opens onto
this terrace, on the lower floor. The
bench is Kenyan, and the embroidered
cushions are mostly from Turkey and
the Maldives.

249

Left, above Black and white dominate one daughter's bedroom. The zebra-striped fabrics are from Pierre Frey. The small collection of corals on the wall provides touches of colour.

Left, below A bedroom. The wardrobe has been painted with motifs borrowed from the Tricia Guild fabric of the bedspread.

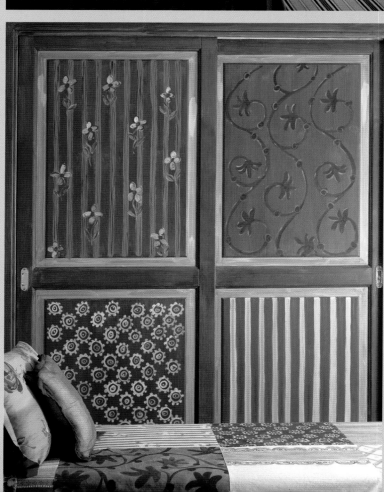

Above Another daughter's bedroom. The turquoise painted wardrobe in this room also uses colours from the patchwork bedspread, which is made from remnants of Designers Guild fabric.

Overleaf An alfresco dining area has been set up on the terrace. The leather chairs were made locally.

Cavallo, France

VILLA KRONOS

Designed by Marianna Gagliardi

Architect Marianna Gagliardi has designed a sophisticated and elegant house in Baia di Zeri, on the Corsican island of Cavallo, for married friends of hers from Florence. The villa is built around a pre-existing wooden structure designed by the French architect Jacques Roque in the 1960s. It has been christened Kronos, meaning 'time', and is virtually monochromatic. The interior is enlivened with a few expertly chosen pieces of furniture and decorated with natural materials and fabrics. This artful simplicity allows the Mediterranean landscape, the sweet-scented maquis, the sea and the sky to become part of the house.

Right The beach terrace is built on several levels, like the deck of a ship.

Left The master bedroom. An early twentieth-century model of a sailing ship stands in front of the full-length windows, which open onto the Baia di Zeri.

Opposite The living room has glass walls which slide out of sight. Outside the window, an ocean-liner-style deck chair.

Overleaf A view of the house from the beach at night.

Capri, Italy

J.K. PLACE

Exterior and interior design by Michele Bönan

When the Florentine architect Michele Bönan made radical alterations to the legendary Palatium hotel on Capri, he created a venue that is destined to achieve mythical status in its own right. Perched above Marina Grande, J.K. Place's decorative scheme is a treasure trove of mementoes, references, cultural echoes and artefacts which call to mind key personalities in the island's history: from the nineteenth-century bronze sphinx on the terrace, which is reminiscent of the magical Villa San Michele, and the portraits of the many famous people who have climbed Capri's steep steps, to the colour scheme which imbues the hotel's interiors with a flavour of the sea and island life.

Above The pure white façade of J.K. Place, set above a shrub-covered rocky headland, looks out over an enchanting seascape beyond Marina Grande, the principal landing place on the island.

Right The terrace overlooks the sea, with Mount Vesuvius looming in the distance. The bronze sphinx is in the foreground.

One of the hotel's reception rooms. The sofas and armchairs were made by expert craftsmen from designs by Michele Bönan. The cobalt blue of the walls, the porthole windows which soften the light, and the Doric columns create an elegant nautical atmosphere which is reminiscent of the eclectic sophistication of noble Neapolitan houses in the eighteenth and nineteenth centuries.

Details such as vases and orchids
contribute to the Mediterranean decor.

263

Opposite and above The hotel has twenty-two bedrooms. In these two rooms, the armchairs and the bench at the end of the bed were designed by Michele Bönan, while the appliqué is by Estro.

Two 3-metre-high (10-foot) Chinese vases are a feature of the restaurant bar. The tables and armchairs were made from Bönan's designs. The photograph on the wall is by Massimo Listri.

Above The armchairs in this bedroom were designed by Bönan. The fabric on the walls is from Dedar. Sunshine yellow is another of the colours in Bönan's lively palette that emphasizes the Mediterranean setting, as does the classical symmetry of the louvred doors.

Overleaf The late nineteenth-century bronze sphinx facing towards the Gulf of Naples is silhouetted against the purplish-blue blush of the evening sky. The sphinx has been part of the hotel since before the restoration.

TITA BEI'S HOUSE

In Ramatuelle, in a quiet corner of Provence, a typical house clinging to the rock has regained its true spirit thanks to the dedication of its owner, who has restored its lively combination of elements, layered and blended over time. Everything is back in its rightful place: wrought-iron furniture, simple folding tables and chairs, and Provençal fabrics fill the rooms which, in turn, are linked by short, steep staircases and spread over several levels according to their own haphazard logic.

Above The original door to the street.

Opposite The staircase leading to the entrance.

Opposite A small window cut out of the ancient wall.

Above, left The table in the living room is covered with Provençal fabrics and laid with Afghan glasses.

Above, right Another area has been set aside for dining and relaxation. The sofa built into the wall is covered with Indian handicrafts and fabrics recycled from typical 1960s Saint-Tropez clothes.

One guest bedroom features a throne-like handcrafted Tuscan chair (in the foreground, to the right) and a zebra-skin rug.

Right, above The master bedroom has an old checked floor, a large Spanish terracotta storage jar, and a folding table and chair which came from an antiques market.

Right, below Another guest bedroom. The elegant wrought-iron headboard of the bed is an old backrest from a bench.

Sorrento, Italy

VILLA TRITONE

Perched above the sea, Villa Tritone was built in 1888 by the Calabrian Count Giovanni Labonia of Bocchigliero on the ruins of the Roman house of Agrippa Postumus (grandson of Emperor Augustus) and a thirteenth-century monastery. The villa has welcomed many notable guests over the years, including Benedetto Croce, Henrik Ibsen, Umberto of Savoy, Palmiro Togliatti and, more recently, Riccardo Muti, Rudolf Nureyev, Lina Wertmüller and Adriano Celentano. The current owners, Rita and Mariano Pane, have looked after this historical, artistic and natural masterpiece with love and meticulous care since the 1970s.

Left The garden wall masks a sheer drop down to the sea. From here one can enjoy the breathtaking panorama of the Gulf of Naples, including the profile of Capri, Punta di Scutolo promontory and the silhouette of Mount Vesuvius. The herm sculpture is by Lawrence Alma-Tadema.

Opposite Villa Tritone was built on a spur of tufa rock and is surrounded by extensive parkland.

The splendid garden was further improved by the American-born publishing magnate William Waldorf Astor, who bought the villa from Giovanni Labonia. He introduced rare plants and romantic pathways, and adorned it with statues and Roman remains such as columns and fountains.

The ornate wall of the belvedere
features herms which were sculpted by
Alma-Tadema in the style of the period.

Opposite The majestic palace has load-bearing tufa walls with arches and vaults, decorated stucco ceilings, marble columns and floors. It has a notable collection of archaeological finds.

Above, left Greco-Roman vases and small sculptures are displayed on a mantelpiece.

Above, right The columns in the foreground are Roman. Through the doorway is the study where the philosopher Benedetto Croce worked when he resided at the villa between 5 December 1942 and 20 January 1945.

This magnificent bedroom still preserves intact the eclectic atmosphere of nineteenth-century aristocratic palaces on the Amalfi Coast. The two display cabinets by the windows contain curios, devotional objects and archaeological finds. Antique maiolica tiles cover the floor.

Opposite The leafy avenue of *Chamaedorea* palms has a pergola covered with *Rosa banksiae* climbing roses.

Above, left This sixteenth-century fountain was made from architectural fragments such as French marble, heraldic coats of arms and antique bronzes.

Above, right A Paleo-Christian sarcophagus depicting a married couple is set in front of a wall with reticulated brickwork.

Saint-Tropez, France

LP'S HOUSE

Designed by Michele Bönan

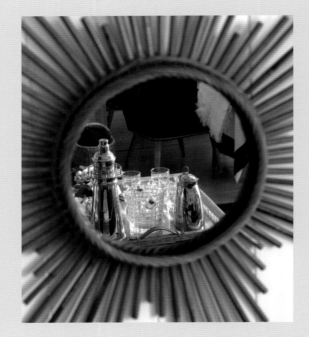

Left Detail of a mirror found at a flea market in Saint-Tropez.

Right The living room on the top floor. The walls are covered with white wooden panelling. The low table in the foreground, which resembles a large ship's trunk, was designed by Michele Bönan.

This former fishermen's cottage and Rothschild-family property overlooking the harbour of Saint-Tropez was gutted and completely remodelled by the Florentine architect Michele Bönan for a Friulian couple, who are also ardent art collectors. Its new owners wanted to have a home with panoramic views where they could enjoy the sparkling climate of the Côte d'Azur and memories of its golden age. In the new rooms, which are organized over four floors and closely resemble the interior spaces of a boat, the guiding principle of the decoration is a 'sentimental education' in nautical themes. The house is filled with maritime objects and colours, and items designed to make it feel like a ship afloat on a tide of memories.

The dining area of the living room.
All the furniture was designed by Bönan.

289

In the master bedroom, the cushions
and the rug are decorated with Michele
Bönan's logo.

Right, above This corner of the living room on the top floor has a colonial feel.

Right, below Another lounge downstairs.

The walls in one bathroom are covered with wood panelling painted blue and white.

The double bed in the master bedroom was a bespoke design.

Above A detail of the upstairs living room. The gouache in the style of Gio Ponti dates from the 1930s.

Right The upstairs living room and corridor.

VILLA KERYLOS

Designed by Emmanuel Pontremoli

Greek-style classicism has left few traces in France, but a villa in the seaside town of Beaulieu, on the Côte d'Azur, is very much an exception to this rule. Villa Kerylos, which is open to visitors, was a dream made reality by Théodore Reinach, an archaeologist, philologist, mathematician, politician and patron of the arts. It was designed in the early twentieth century by the architect Emmanuel Pontremoli, who modelled it on the noble houses of the second century BC on the island of Delos but was adamant that it should not be a mere copy. The house was intended as an educational journey into classical antiquity, and as a fascinating diorama of an idealized Greco-Roman era. Not only were the architecture, decoration and artworks based on historical models, but every aspect of life in the house conformed with knowledge of the period – to such a degree that every room in the villa was given a Greek name which evoked a specific everyday activity from that fascinating golden age.

Left A detail of the Andron, the main reception hall of the villa.

Right A view of Villa Kerylos from the sea, surrounded by its terraced garden. Emmanuel Pontremoli wanted to create the impression that the palace had sprung up almost spontaneously among the trees.

Above Another detail of the Andron showing the marble columns.

Left The library has east-facing windows which make reading in the morning easier. The tall writing desks are intended for work to be done standing up and for the consultation of large books. Roman chairs made from leather share the space with Greek vases and artefacts from the period between the 6th and 1st centuries BC. Esoteric Greek symbols are reproduced in the mosaic floor.

Overleaf The Andron. This is where Reinach loved to hold conversations while he sat on a throne-like chair. The columns and walls are finished in marble. Glass and bronze lamps hang from the coffered teak ceiling.

The Ornitès, or Chambre aux Oiseaux, was Madame Reinach's room. It is decorated in many shades of blue and with swan and peacock motifs. These sacred creatures were particular favourites of the goddess Hera, wife of Zeus.

Right The Nikäi, Madame Reinach's private bathroom.

Opposite The Ornitès again, with Madame Reinach's bed.

Left Details of the patterns which decorate the walls and floors of the room of Triptolemus.

Opposite The room of Triptolemus. The walls are frescoed with branches of ivy and olive trees, while the mosaic on the floor depicts the mythological Triptolemus scattering grain across the world.

Above Detail, showing a small bronze statue of a serpent.

Right The Triklinos, or Banqueting Room. Reinach loved to serve his legendary dinners here on terracotta plates, which were reproductions of originals from the 6th century BC, and with Roman-style blown-glass goblets. His guests, dressed in tunics, dined while reclining on the long couches.

Above A peristyle of twelve Doric columns in white Carrara marble forms the boundary of the patio. Reinach liked to stroll around here and muse upon his many interests.

Right Pillars frame a view of the beautiful Côte d'Azur sea.

FERNANDO BOTERO AND SOPHIA VARI'S HOUSE

Designed by Katerina Tsigarida
Garden by Dennis Riedrimont

Two great contemporary artists, the Colombian Fernando Botero and his Greek-Hungarian wife Sophia Vari, found the home they had been searching for near Athens, on an island off the Attica coast. With the assistance of Katerina Tsigarida, a young architect from Thessaloniki, Fernando and Sophia have modified the house to their own tastes, creating a fluid succession of cube-like spaces of varying heights, and picturesque arcades and patios which give a rhythm to the exterior. The predominantly white interior contains select pieces of elegant furniture, design classics displayed next to pre-Columbian sculptures, Greek vases, and works of art by the owners. The villa is surrounded by a splendid Mediterranean garden designed by the landscape architect Dennis Riedrimont.

Left The rear façade of the house. The arches are reflected in the water of the deck-level swimming pool.

Opposite The main entrance. The watercolour *Etude* by Fernando Botero can be seen in the background.

Overleaf Another view of the rear façade of the building at night. The lounges and the alfresco dining area in the arcade are lit up.

A Rio Chaise Longue designed by Oscar Niemeyer and made by Fasem is in the living room.

Right On the table is a sculpture by
Sophia Vari. A portrait of Sophia Vari
painted by Botero hangs on the wall.

Opposite The interior dining room seen
from the living room. Black lacquered
chairs by Josef Hoffmann are arranged
around the table. In the foreground is
the fireplace, decorated with a marble
relief by Sophia Vari.

319

Three pre-Columbian sculptures are displayed on a table by Francesco Soro, with the marble relief by Sophia Vari in the background.

Above The living room. *La plage* by
Fernando Botero hangs above the sofa.
The table is by Francis Arsène.

Overleaf A view of the arcade and the
garden.

The master bedroom is in plain white.

One of the rooms opens onto this
arcade, with a hammock in the garden
beyond.

Botero's atelier is in a separate building,
surrounded by enormous olive trees
which are many centuries old.

Beaulieu, France

VILLA GIACHERO

Designed by Giacomo Passera

The turret of an Art Nouveau villa stands out against the blue sky, with views down to the harbour of Beaulieu and the electric blue of the French Mediterranean. The architect Giacomo Passera has redesigned the building for a successful plastic surgeon from Turin. He has not altered the original layout but has lightened the interiors by using vibrant colours inspired by Matisse and by the Mediterranean. He has also introduced elegant pieces in the style of Jean Cocteau, and included skilful references to the Côte d'Azur's golden age, to the chic style of interior designer Jean-Michel Frank, and to the clean lines of the 1940s.

Left A gesso plinth and vase from the 1940s in the entrance hall.

Opposite Wicker armchairs on the balcony overlooking the harbour of Beaulieu.

Left, above The dining room has Matisse-blue walls and white plaster moulding. A series of eighteenth-century Chinese watercolours is framed by the plaster panelling.

Left, below The Venetian mirror above the fireplace dates from the 1930s. Two Murano glass candleholders are displayed on the mantelpiece.

The oval lounge. In front of the Napoleon III marble fireplace are two eighteenth-century *Duchesse brisée* armchairs covered with a 1950s fabric. Two white Art Deco side tables decorated with gilded balls stand on either side of the fireplace.

Opposite Plasterwork and a gesso panel decorate the living room. The rug was made from a design by David Hockney.

Above, left The walls of the entrance hall are painted a mint green.

Above, right The entrance hall again, with the doorway to the dining room.

Above, left The walls of the study feature
an unusual oak-panel-effect wallpaper
from Nobilis, inspired by 1940s wood
panelling. The damask-covered
armchairs and the bronze and marble
coffee table date from the 1940s, while
the English writing desk is from the
1930s. On the floor is a coir mat.

Above, right A closer view of the fireplace
in the study.

Opposite The corridor is lit by a Murano
glass chandelier and by Barovier
wall-mounted lights from the 1940s.
A section of hand-painted nineteenth-
century wallpaper can be seen in the
background. Both the wrought-iron
console table and the mirror above it
are from the 1940s.

Left The bathroom.

Opposite The master bedroom. The four-poster bed has curtains made from double-sided fabric.

Overleaf A view of the turret at night.

Stromboli, Italy

VILLA TRICLINIO

Designed by Ezio Riva

This mansion house with views over the Gulf of Tigullio has been given a wonderfully theatrical redesign by Ezio Riva. Its original core consists of two watchtowers dating from 1145. Riva has brought these elegant spaces between the marble columns and vaulted ceilings to life with impressive effects, skilfully juxtaposing works by famous artists with outstanding pieces of furniture.

Left A window grille made from a design by the owner and inspired by Gaudí.

Opposite A *Barocco* armchair from the Cyrus Company on the terrace of the master bedroom.

Above Luca Pignatelli's ***Aphrodite*** hangs
above the sofa in the living room. In
the background, a frame from Avallone
rests on the floor.

Left A marble-topped table designed by
the owner is positioned between marble
columns. A sculpture by Alexandra de
Lazareff is displayed on the table.

Left, above A bedroom.

Left, below The bathroom. The painting is by Giovanni Sesia, who lives and works in Magenta, Milan, while the furniture is from Michel Haillard's Wunderkammer *Kibbutz*. The lantern is Moroccan, and the bronze sculpture on the stone washbasin is by Novello Finotti. The owner made the hanging lamp by using a slab of crystal as a diffuser.

Opposite The guest bedroom features a collection of antique weapons displayed high up on the wall.

The bathroom and the master bedroom.
The gold mosaics on the walls and the
floor date from the nineteenth century.

Nice, France

ROCHE AZURE

Interior design by Angelo Brignolli and Antonio Feraboli

Angelo Brignolli and Antonio Feraboli of Studio Linea have added two glass-enclosed verandas, currently used as a kitchen and a gymnasium, to an early twentieth-century villa on a hillside overlooking Nice. The interiors have been redesigned for a young couple with children who wanted to live in elegant, modern spaces within a traditional structure, and to enjoy the wide panoramic views of the Côte d'Azur.

Above The swimming pool and terraced garden of Roche Azure. A solarium has been created on the parterre.

Right The view from the hill, looking out over Nice harbour.

Left, above The entrance hall beyond the portico with its columns and tympanum has been returned to its original glory. The plasterwork, marble floor, and glass and wrought-iron gate were restored with the assistance of architect Paolo Guarneri.

Left, below Two Khmer sculptures stand guard on either side of the folding door designed by Angelo Brignolli and Antonio Feraboli.

Opposite A view of the villa with its columned portico at night. The swimming pool is in the foreground.

Above The master bedroom. The cupboards, armchairs and pouf were all designed specially for this television corner.

Left The dining room. The table and lacquered wood panelling were made from designs by Brignolli and Feraboli. The painting above the fireplace is by Paolo Sistilli. The table is laid with shells instead of plates, and the centrepiece is made from vine roots.

Above Antonio Mazzetti's photopainting of a sculpture by Jean Dubuffet can be seen above the sofa beyond the half-open doors of the lounge.

Right Another photopainting by Mazzetti of Santiago Calatrava's Milwaukee Art Museum hangs in the living room. The lamps with wenge wood bases were inspired by Umberto Boccioni and designed by Brignolli and Feraboli. The floor is covered with white Carrara marble tiles interspersed with small squares of Belgian black marble.

Above and opposite Two verandas have been added to the main body of the villa, one of which has been equipped as a gym.

Overleaf A fiery sunset forms the
backdrop to the kitchen veranda.

On the cover: (*front*) Villa Olivetta, Portofino, Italy; (*back*) Casa Catastini, Elba, Italy

Translated from the Italian *Casa Mediterranea* by Grace Crerar-Bromelow

First published in the United Kingdom in 2009 by Thames & Hudson Ltd, 181A High Holborn, London WC1V 7QX

www.thamesandhudson.com

First published in 2009 in hardcover in the United States of America by Thames & Hudson Inc., 500 Fifth Avenue, New York, New York 10110

thamesandhudsonusa.com

Original edition © 2009 Magnus Edizioni Srl, Udine
Illustrations © 2009 Massimo Listri
This edition © 2009 Thames & Hudson, London

British Library Cataloguing-in-Publication Data
A catalogue record for this book is available from the British Library

Library of Congress Catalog Card Number 2009901944

ISBN 978-0-500-51494-8

Printed and bound in Italy